W0259398

Kikyō

COMING HOME TO POWELL STREET

Kikyō

COMING HOME TO POWELL STREET

TAMIO WAKAYAMA

ORAL HISTORIES GATHERED AND EDITED BY

LINDA UYEHARA HOFFMAN

AFTERWORD BY

PAUL WONG

HARBOUR PUBLISHING / MADEIRA PARK

SU PRESS / KOBE

Copyright © 1992 by Tamio Wakayama

All rights reserved

Harbour Publishing Co. Ltd., P.O. Box 219 Madeira Park, BC Canada V0N 2H0

SU Press, 1-13 Ikuta-cho I-chome, Chuo-ku, Kobe 651, Japan

Written and published with the assistance of the Canada Council; the Government of British Columbia, Tourism and Ministry Responsible for Culture, Cultural Services Branch; the Department of the Secretary of State, Multiculturalism and Citizenship Canada; the Japanese Canadian Redress Foundation; the Powell Street Festival Society; the Japanese Canadian Citizens' Association History Preservation Committee.

Cover photograph (Linda Uyehara Hoffman, Katari Taiko, 1981) by Tamio Wakayama

Cover design, page design and type by Roger Handling, Glassford Design Studios

Japanese calligraphy by Junko Hayashi

Kikyō logo type by Hubert Keeven

Printed and bound in Canada

Canadian Cataloguing in Publication Data

Wakayama, Tamio.

Kikyō

ISBN 1-55017-062-7

1. Powell Street Festival (Vancouver, B.C.). 2. Japanese Canadians—British Columbia— Vancouver.* I. Title.

FC3847.9.J3W34 1992 971.1'33004956

F1089.5.V22W34 1992 C92-091165-X

To the Issei and especially to my late mother, Kinu Abe Wakayama, who never did get to see the Powell Street Festival.

CONTENTS

帰郷

INTRODUCTION

I was born in 1941, the sixth and final offspring of an immigrant couple who had left a small fishing village in Kyushu to fulfill their dream of riches in the New World. With savings scrimped from years of toil in the logging industry, my father had managed to purchase an unassuming two-storey structure on the Lougheed Highway some twenty miles due east of Powell Street and Little Tokyo. We lived on the second floor while the first was reserved for the family business: a grocery store in the front, and in the back, large vats for the making of tofu. Once or twice a week my father would load up the new Ford truck to make his round of deliveries either to Powell Street or to neighbouring farms and families. The dream was finally becoming a reality.

The dream ended with the bombing of Pearl Harbor. In a few short months our land, our house, the tofu business, the prized Ford—the accumulated wealth of a lifetime's labour—was gone. Branded as Enemy Aliens in our own land, we were herded into the cattle stalls of Hastings Park, while numerous relocation camps were being hastily constructed in the remote interior to hold the uprooted coastal community of Japanese Canadians. Eventually we were removed to Tashme, the largest of these camps, located near the town of Hope.

When the camps closed at the end of the war, my parents resisted the federal government's effort to "repatriate" all Japanese Canadians to Japan and instead, we suffered a lesser banishment to a small rural community in southwestern Ontario. After spending a year working on a fruit farm on the shores of Lake Erie, we bought a small, ramshackle house in the black ghetto of Chatham which had been, at one time, a terminus of the underground railway for runaway slaves. We were one of the fortunate few to own our own home; a neighbouring family of six could only find an abandoned chicken coop. My father, like most of the new arrivals, worked at a nearby fertilizer factory and tannery that would, on breezeless summer days, blanket the entire city with the stench billowing from its tall brick smokestack.

Steveston, Little Tokyo, all our vibrant communities of the prewar days were becoming a distant memory. In the isolation of our exodus east of the Rockies, we would sorely miss these centres, which had nurtured self-esteem and offered refuge from the racism that had plagued the Nikkei since the arrival of the first Japanese immigrant to Canada. The sudden uprooting and incarceration of our community was an appalling tragedy but we, the children of the dispossessed, know the greater damage to our individual and collective psyche occurred in the lonely years of exile.

We entered a world still dominated by the new and powerful phenomenon of mass culture. Hollywood had led the way, implanting in the public eye a vision of World War Two as a titanic clash of Good and Evil. As Enemy Aliens we were the very embodiment of racial evil, and inevitably, many of the towns and cities in our eastward migration fought to bar us from their gates. The state, abetted by the crushing weight of mass media, had effected policies that were nothing less than cultural genocide.

Much of my own life has been spent in coming to terms with the memory of growing up in Chatham. I remember the cries of "Jap go home" and a judo teacher who warded off his tormentors with a perfectly executed series of hip and shoulder throws. I remember my own battles to and from school, fought with little skill and even lesser glory. I remember the first day of classes and the ordeal of registration—sitting at my desk, the lone Asian, waiting in agony for the moment when I would have to interrupt the litany of genteel white names and voice aloud the alien syllables of my father's name. I remember going to the movies with my friend Keibo to watch John Wayne repel wave after wave of the treacherous yellow hordes. Keibo fled the theatre screaming "Japs, Japs, Japs." I stayed, and in my childhood memory John Wayne became enshrined as the ultimate, immutable icon of noble manhood. But he was clearly beyond the reach of an Enemy Alien and my sense of self fell in the cracks of these contradictions.

My long journey from exile and alienation began in the early sixties, when I turned on the TV to witness a spectacle unfolding at a small, segregated diner in Danville, Virginia. With raw eggs and Coke streaming down their faces, black youth sat calmly at the forbidden lunch counter in a maelstrom of racial hate and violence. From the deep but yet unnamed echoes of my own past came the compelling need to go South.

In the early evening of Sunday, September 10, 1963, I arrived in Birmingham, Alabama, eleven hours after four black children had been killed in a bombing of a church basement. At the Gaston Motel, the assembly point for the civil rights workers arriving from all parts of the nation, I attached myself to the dungaree-clad members of Snick, the Student Nonviolent Coordinating Committee. They were the scruffy and rebellious youth arm of the civil rights movement, the shock troops who were challenging the entrenched power of some of the most lethal counties of the Black Belt South.

After the funeral for the young victims of the bombing, I drove the leadership of Snick back to their headquarters in Atlanta. My car was a rare asset for the impoverished organization so I carried on as a chauffeur, ferrying people to and from mass rallies, sit-ins and the city jail. When my meagre savings ran out I was put on the payroll with a subsistence allowance of $25 a week.

Snick was in the midst of a fierce campaign to desegregate all the restaurants in Atlanta's downtown core. Since most of our office staff were already behind bars, there was no one left to produce a flyer for an upcoming mass rally to recruit fresh troops for the sit-ins. I went down to the layout room of the *Student Voice*, our weekly newspaper, and designed my first poster with the lines "THE FACE OF ATLANTA—HELP CHANGE IT" framing a striking head shot of a Klansman in full regalia, grimacing from the window of a white-only diner.

More and more of my time was spent in the layout room where I worked with the images of Danny Lyon, a New York photographer whose stunning portfolio of the movement launched an illustrious career. With his encouragement and the generous loan of his backup Nikon, I first began to explore my own photographic vision. Other photographers came down from the North to document Snick projects throughout the deep South, and despite my protests, I was delegated to stay in Atlanta to administer the operations. We converted the women's bathroom to a darkroom (feminism was still in its infancy) and after a one-hour crash course in the chemical mysteries of the medium, I was left alone to begin processing the hundreds of rolls of film that would be shot over that eventful summer. The countless hours spent in that tiny sweltering room, with huge rats scurrying unseen beneath my feet, proved to be an invaluable training ground for my future development.

I finally entered the field when one of our photographers in Mississippi returned to California after suffering his third beating and loss of equipment at the hands of an enraged mob. I drove to Neshoba County, where three civil rights workers had been killed that summer, and in the terror and beauty of the Black Belt South, I learned to be a photographer.

I spent two years in the South and grew immeasurably in one of the brightest moments of American life. The civil rights movement had inspired a generation of North American youth and altered their lives forever. And for a young, naive Japanese Canadian seeking to re-create his identity, the moment was especially luminous, for the black revolution was, in essence, a revolution of self. The growing cry of Black is Beautiful was aimed directly at the psychic core of segregated America where White was the ultimate moral and aesthetic standard and Black was the colour of the other, the lesser being. The demand of Black Power was more an inward call to radically transform the downtrodden sense of self inherited from a century of slavery and oppression; only then could political equality be achieved and made meaningful. This quest would illuminate the remainder of my own journey and, armed with the growing power of a new medium, I returned to explore the social landscape of my own country.

The tidal wave of youthful idealism that had started in the South was now sweeping across the border. For the past week, the brutalization of the marchers en route to Selma, Alabama had been major news, and I was called to advise a group of students at the University of Toronto who wanted to add their voice to the growing worldwide protest. The next morning, about twenty members of the Student Union for Peace Action sat down on the snowy pavement in front of the American Consulate. By nightfall, the normally staid city of Toronto was electrified and involved: the sidewalk was choked with new arrivals, hauling sleeping bags for an all-night vigil; a society matron strolling by took off her fur coat and draped it over a shivering demonstrator; a delivery truck from nearby Chinatown stopped to unload buckets of chow mein and sweet and sour ribs. The demonstration went on for days and nights until the situation in Selma was finally resolved.

Encouraged by the stunning success of this demonstration, the organizers planned to mobilize the dispossessed of Canada in the urban slum of Toronto's Cabbagetown, Native reserves in Saskatchewan, and the gentle communities of Doukhobors in the Kootenay Valley. I lived in these communities, photographing a political process that was, for me, a pale imitation of the life-and-death struggles of the movement in the South. Without the sustaining power of the grass roots, these projects were doomed to be short-lived and yet, when this ersatz movement finally passed away, I was devastated by the loss, for I sensed it was the end of an era.

The decade of the sixties, which had begun with the promise of a new millennium, was now fading into the banalities of flower power and the indulgences of the drug culture. In the South, the Black movement, disillusioned with the snail's pace of political change and the unremitting violence, was becoming more inward looking, their focus shifting now to Black nationalism and their African heritage. Seeking new directions for myself, I turned to Japan, which was to be the final bridge that brought me back to Powell Street.

I arrived in Tokyo, and with the sudden immersion in a sea of Asians came the startling realization that I was no longer a visible minority. But the novel and not unpleasant sense of anonymity ended once I began to speak in the almost forgotten and largely incomprehensible Japanese learned from my parents. Despite the immense barriers of language and culture, I was graciously welcomed to the ancestral land, a prodigal son returning home. And in my travels through the many islands of Japan, I looked everywhere for the evil yellow hordes of my childhood memory but could only find the proud and energetic Japanese, inheritors of an ancient culture and builders of the vaunted miracle of modern Japan.

I returned to Tokyo and in the short walk from the subway station to my adopted home in Ogikubo, I literally ran into Lita, who was to be my mentor and constant companion for the remainder of my stay. She was a young Taiwanese student of eastern religions but her English, flavoured with a slight Boston accent from years of study at Radcliffe, was impeccable. It was a relief to speak freely again in English and Lita herself was a total delight, an effervescent child-woman who could change, in an instant, from Taiwanese teeny-bopper to ancient Asian mystic.

One day Lita came home in a rage: she had spent the long subway ride from her university fighting off the aggressive advances of a fellow exchange student from Cambridge. Her diatribe on the ugly American—his arrogance, his ungainly size, his odour, his repulsive white flesh like puffy bread dough—was an epiphany. I was hearing a sweeping reversal of familiar stereotypes, a feminine Asian perspective that challenged the sacrosanct neo-classic WASP male of my childhood memory ... John Wayne, a rank Pillsbury Doughboy?

That evening, the false idols of the past toppled forever in the flickering light of our favourite Tokyo movie house, featuring three samurai epics for a mere 500 yen. As the heroes of the Japanese pantheon came to life, I had a sudden vision of John Wayne locked in mortal combat with Zatoichi, the legendary blind swordsman. It was all so simple. Idols are not immutable but mere expressions of a cultural ethos. There are thousands of them and one is probably as good as another. It really was true—the icons of beauty and noble manhood, like racism itself, exist solely in the eyes of the beholder. And from the dark side of the Land of the Rising Sun, where cultural pride and homogeneity are eclipsed by arrogance and xenophobia, came the added discovery that racism is as universal as it is arbitrary.

My year-long pilgrimage was coming to an end. The fertile ancestral soil had yielded a new and growing acceptance of a cultural heritage too long denied but now, in the stultifying heat of the approaching summer, I needed to escape these narrow, claustrophobic islands with their endless procession of people, all stamped from the same physical mold. In my longing for the great and cleansing scale of the Canadian landscape and the rich diversity of its social mosaic, I realized that, for better or worse, my identity had been forged forever in the crucible of my native land. I left for home, leaving behind the worn-out icon of the Enemy Alien.

Before flying back to Toronto, I stopped over in Vancouver where I met an old friend who whisked me off to the wilds of Thurlow Island. Our float plane gently came to rest on the waters of a crystalline lake, set like a jewel in the virgin rain forest, and I entered the perfect realization of all of my fantasies during the dog days of Tokyo summer. The island became a magnet that drew me back each summer until one year, the thought of enduring yet another cold and dreary eastern winter, forced my final return to the West Coast.

Eventually I relocated my studio in Vancouver's downtown eastside, a few blocks from Powell Street. One day I received a letter from my mother and after fruitless hours of translation, I walked over to the nearby office of Language Aid for Immigrant Societies. The mysteries of the letter were revealed by Michiko, a vivaciously beautiful new arrival from Nagasaki. After hearing of my interest in the *shakuhachi*, the ethereal Japanese bamboo flute, she sent me down the street to Tonari Gumi. The senior citizens drop-in centre was in the middle of a raucous, bilingual Bingo game—"B eight, bee hachi"—and after one white-haired *obāchan* filled her line, I went over and met Take, one of the founders of Tonari Gumi and a genuine master of the *shakuhachi*. I was finally back on Powell Street.

I entered a community still largely dormant after the great shocks of the war years. The catalyst of its awakening was people like Michiko and Take, a new breed of immigrants who had left the strictures of their rigid society to find, in this open land, the freedom to develop their irrepressible individuality. In the dingy rooms of Language Aid and Tonari Gumi, they helped ease the isolation of those who had suffered most from the wartime uprooting, the elderly Issei. These centres became the forum of a new dialogue between the generations—a place for the Sansei to forge vital linkages to their history and culture—and from this dialogue arose the opening challenges to the comfortable assumptions of history that sought to justify the injustices of the war years under the guise of national security. When the hollowness of these assumptions was fully revealed, the community went on to press for a just resolution of their historic claim for redress.

On Powell Street, a new coalition was rapidly growing around the nucleus of recent immigrants. For those of us Canadian-born, working with our ethnic peers was an unfamiliar experience and our initial encounters had the awkward hesitancy of a meeting of strangers—our denial of self had led inevitably to a rejection of each other. The estrangement, however, quickly dissipated in the buoyant energy of our immigrant allies, their proud and unassuming sense of themselves as Japanese serving as a beacon to our ethnic roots. And the lives of the Issei, the tough and tenacious generation of pioneers, illuminated the worthiness of our historic legacy. Our communal instinct, liberated from its long suppression, spawned a dream to recreate the vitality that had once flowed through the community of Little Tokyo.

The surging crosscurrents of our awakening finally came together in the bright sun of a summer's weekend when the *taiko* drumbeats of the first Powell Street Festival echoed across Oppenheimer Park. For the first time since the war years, the dispersed Nikkei community was reunited on the grounds where an older generation had once gathered to enact its rituals and acclaim its heroes. We came not as victims but as celebrants of our victory over a vicious racism that had sought our removal from these lands. In the 100th year since the arrival of the first Japanese immigrant to Canada, we had come home to Powell Street.

To explore the undercurrents of historic memory that have nurtured fifteen years of the Powell Street Festival, the images in this book have had to venture beyond the limits of documentary photography to find their proper home in the realm of metaphor and myth. They and their accompanying voices, orchestrated from nearly a hundred interviews of Festival participants, are an allegory of renewal: the awakening and empowerment of a new generation of Nikkei who came home to the tattered remains of Little Tokyo to recreate a communal memory perverted by a century of racism.

The images are also myth, for their reflections of joyful energy belie the present state of our community in the post-redress period. Despite the tremendous outpouring of energy and commitment that went into the redress struggle, the promise of a united and revitalized community has largely failed to materialize. In our relentless pursuit of our political goals we somehow lost sight of the overriding need to heal ourselves. Our own fragility was forgotten in the metaphysical abstraction of a just and honourable resolution, and we became our own worst enemy. We did not achieve full and consensual participation in the redress process, nor did we exercise enough care to ensure each contribution was respected and recognized. In 1992, the 50th anniversary of the wartime uprooting, we are a community divided and still in search of itself.

In many ways redress was an aborted process. The actual announcement by Parliament on September 22, 1988, granting formal apology and financial compensation to the victims of the wartime injustices, came shortly after the passage of a similar resolution in the American Congress. The American victory was the result of a skilled and vigorous redress movement that predated ours by a full decade. Our American allies had the time to struggle through their internal strife to arrive at synthesis and resolution. They achieved a rebirth of community through such events as the deeply moving and cathartic Congressional hearings where ordinary men and women gave public witness to their suffering and outrage. Our own victory came too quickly, and we lost a unique opportunity to cauterize our deep historic wounds through the heat of political battle.

My images are indeed myth, but the importance of myth lies not in its correspondence with reality, but rather with its creation of vision, the proverbial light to lead us to the end of a dark tunnel. In the aftermath of redress we are in need of vision, now more than ever.

The treatment of Japanese Canadians during the war years was a savage act of institutionalized racism that is, except for the treatment of the aboriginal peoples, unparalleled in Canadian history. The aftershocks of the upheaval will continue to roll through present and future generations of Japanese Canadians. Today the Nikkei are an endangered species. Our present high rate of intermarriage is not only a striking anomaly in comparison with other ethnic groups but also, taken to its logical conclusion, it will render meaningless the very concept of Japanese Canadians as a distinct and definable community. The question we are struggling with is not the intrusive and ultimately racist one of racial purity: we are not advocating a choice of mates. But we are dealing with the real dilemma of whether we have gained enough distance from our alienation to make a free choice.

The voices in this book have probed these and other questions with remarkable candour and eloquence. Beneath the colourful *kimonos*, the visceral beat of *taiko* and the tantalizing aroma of *teriyaki* salmon, is a serious and passionate attempt to affirm our cultural legacy and to lay the groundwork for our future. For many, the Festival has and will continue to serve as a joyous starting point in the long journey to self-discovery. For those who have yet to cross the borders of their alienation, we leave the vision of the Powell Street Festival and the myth and metaphor of *Kikyō*—in coming home to Powell Street we have found a heritage that is worthy of respect and public celebration.

Tamio Wakayama

June 1992

歸鄉

LITTLE TOKYO

I can still remember going to those baseball games on Powell Street with my father. He'd be sitting with his friends and they'd laugh and talk and, of course, criticize the umpire. And it was like seeing my father a completely different person. He wasn't the master of the house when he was there; he was just a young man with his friends. He was funny and fun to be with, and if I moaned and said I was bored, he'd give me a nickel, and I could go get an ice cream cone which was very rare in those Depression days.

Oh, my father followed the Asahi team all over and he knew every single player by name. Without Powell Street and without those teams, I wonder what life would have been like for someone like him. There was so little joy in their lives—for my father, baseball was his only real joy. I don't know whether he was a rarity or whether all Issei men felt that strongly about the Asahi team. I'm sure some of it was that "us against them" feeling—we were the runts, but we could outrun them.

Midge Ayukawa

Growing up on Powell Street was exciting, but Christmas and New Year's were particularly so. The stores were all decorated with Christmas things. And I'd take my brother and we'd go window shopping—you could get everything on Powell Street. But as I got older, I wanted to get shoes from Woodward's because it was much more stylish. And my dad would say, "But Mr. Nabata's a fellow merchant, he supports my business, so you should buy your shoes there." And then Mom would say, because she's a Nisei, she'd say, "Couldn't we meet Shirley halfway? Maybe we'll buy the winter shoes from Nabata's, but maybe she could get the white shoes from Woodward's."

I didn't know how Mom and Dad did it—when we went to bed on the 24th, we had just the Christmas tree, but when we got up on the 25th, there would be all these gifts lined up on a table—one section for me, one section for my sister and one section for my brother. Three Christmas stockings would be hanging on the chimney, and I used to wonder how Santa could come down a narrow chimney like that into a potbelly stove.

Then on the 26th, Boxing Day, my father closed up most of the sections of the store, Kasuga Kashiten, because we had to start making *mochi*. From the 26th to the 31st, we made only *mochi*. And Dad would have extra help with three shifts going. The kitchen was used to cool off the *mochi* so we ate breakfast in a corner, but for lunch and dinner we always crossed Powell Street to the restaurants.

On the 31st, Mother would send me off with these large plates to Star Fish Market, Maikawa's and Hayashi across the street. And at the end of the day, very late on the 31st, these merchants would deliver the *sushi*, *sashimi* and huge *ebi*, and Mother would cook the rest of the festive dishes so everything was prepared for January 1st. And then the store would close for three or four days.

Because I was the oldest, Dad and I would go to the Buddhist church first thing in the morning on January 1st. We'd come home and Mother would have the *ozoni* all ready for us. Young as we were, that was the one morning that Dad would have a little bit of *sake* for the whole family to toast. After that, we never saw him, because he would have his customary rounds to make, and others would be coming to the house, and the place would be full of people all day. The second day, women were allowed to go out if they so wished, but usually they stayed home because they had all the clean-up to do.

But the second day, we kids would go to the western movies. There were Japanese movies too, at the Japanese Language School. Mr. Tsuyuki used to do the dubbing. They weren't talkies, so he'd fill in the dialogue. I think he was evacuated to Tashme and carried on there.

Shirley Kakutani

I landed up on Powell Street in the summer of 1935, helping Rigenda Sumida with housework in the rooming house, making the beds and sweeping up. It was a flophouse in the middle of the Depression.

In those days, the area was marginal and yet prosperous to a degree. It was an established Little Tokyo—nearly all the businesses from about Main Street to Jackson and even beyond were all small local businesses run by Japanese. And people lived around there, some above the stores, some behind, some along Cordova and Alexander Streets and east of there. You didn't have to move beyond that three-four blocks if you didn't want to—entertainment and food, a bookstore, the Japanese bath. There were concerts and theatre and Japanese films, particularly at the Language School.

We started the *New Canadian* over the print shop down on Alexander Street. Then we got two rooms in the New World Hotel and ran the newspaper, overlooking Powell Grounds. The impetus behind starting the newspaper was the struggle for civil rights. It was an expression of political activism. We stayed through all that evacuation period until finally we decided that we had to go too. At the end of August or in September, we packed up everything, including reams and reams of Japanese type, and went to Kaslo. We were among the last to leave.

We sat there and watched the community bleeding away.

Tom Shoyama

When I was growing up, it was pretty rough for us—I remember we used to take pride in the fact that we were the poorest family on Cordova Street. Then when I was four, we moved to Steveston, and I never went back there until 1989 when I played at the Powell Street Festival.

I hadn't been to Vancouver for many years, but I wanted to see Archie, my brother. And all my old friends. Didn't see any. Couldn't find one. But most of all I wanted to see Vancouver. I used to watch the baseball games on Powell Street now and then. I thought it was big, I thought it was huge. But looking at it in 1989, it seemed kind of small. I used to walk up and down Powell Street when I was playing hookey from Japanese School, just about every other day. Everything looked different. Like I was in a foreign place. Even the mountains looked different. I expected to see the Three Sisters just across the inlet. It wasn't there. It was somewhere else. I still don't know where it is.

Roy Miya

歸鄉

THE POWELL STREET FESTIVAL

Japanese festivals…usually you've got one in the springtime, one in the autumn. Where I came from they call it *omikoshi*, what you carry, and to carry the *omikoshi*, you have to be a certain age. In the springtime, I forget what the age was but autumn, age forty-two. At age forty-two, you might get sick or something, so to get the bad stuff away from your inside, you carry the *omikoshi*. Even if you live out of town, say in Tokyo, they come back to carry the *omikoshi*.

They call it *akubarai*, that means to get the spirits out, all the bad things should go out.

Shig Hirai

Maxfli

When I came to Vancouver from New York in 1970, I think I was returning to find my roots. All the time I was in New York, I was totally with non-Japanese people and avoided anything Japanese. Then suddenly, coming to Vancouver, I wanted to figure out what I am. So I went to Powell Street. Here was a street, a little bit rundown, with a Japanese flavour, Japanese restaurants, food shops, but very poor people kind of hanging around and drunk. And it made me feel sad to see the street all forgotten.

So I started this place called Language Aid to help the Japanese senior citizens. I went to the Japanese Canadian organizations for help, and they said, "No, we don't need that kind of assistance, because we take care of our elders." Then when we opened, we were flooded with these old people coming to ask us to write letters to Japan, or they didn't understand letters sent to them by the government, or they wanted to apply for a pension but didn't know how. They were cut off from the rest of the world.

Hearing the incredible stories of their lives, I started getting deeply involved with them. It suddenly started mushrooming—a whole new group of people started coming in. Powell Street seemed like a magnet in those days, pulling all these people in. And one day we decided we should revive that festival they used to have in Little Tokyo, on the Powell Grounds, where they used to play baseball together, hang around, parade, *Obon* festivals—always there were pictures of Powell Street. That's where the action was. We wanted to revive that, bring the people back, and I think that's how the Festival was started.

Michiko Sakata

It was incredible working on that first Festival because I'd never worked with other Sansei before. I was a typical third-generation Japanese Canadian who thought that I was unique and all other Sansei were—well, the guys are boring, the women aren't very attractive. You didn't want to be associated with other Asians at that time because people would lump you into those kinds of categories. When you're growing up, you have all these negative images—from the media, all different sources—of what Nikkei or other Asians are like.

Ken Shikaze

I sort of had this schizoid view of who I was. I thought I was Japanese. Whoever asked me, "Like, what are you?"—which I thought was a really strange question—I told them, "I'm Canadian." "Yeah, I know you're Canadian, but what are you really?" After playing the game a little bit, "Yeah, I'm Japanese." They're trying not to be rude, and I'm trying not to be so sarcastic. I guess my integration is coming really slowly.

My brother and sister have totally denied any kind of cultural tie or identity with Japanese. They shun everything Japanese. My brother won't even buy a Japanese car, I don't think. He'll buy a Sony television because it's the best on the market, but he would rather buy a Ford. To buy a Ford is just sacrilege!

Les Yamada

My concern before the first Festival was "Do they know what they're doing? Do they really understand the background of the area to be able to put on a festival on the Powell Street Grounds?" It was not so much that the organizers of the first Festival were Sansei, it was more, "Do they really understand the community?" The Nisei generation—we all seemed to have similar backgrounds, similar kinds of suffering. Then out of the clear blue sky this Sansei blows in from Toronto. I thought, "Oh, Rick Shiomi. Mary, his older sister, and I went to school together, so I guess he's all right." At the same time, you think, "Does he really know what he's doing?"

Shirley Kakutani

There's nothing to match the first festival. Nothing to match the wonderful insanity that went on. I was in such shock at certain phases of working on it that I used to walk down the streets with my shoelaces untied. I never felt I had time to bend over and tie my shoelaces. I went for days worrying about details because I was functionally inoperative. I was probably having a nervous breakdown without realizing it. You know, when I went into the Festival, I had this sense of competence, but gradually that sense was completely eroded for me. I distrusted all my abilities to handle anything, to make decisions about anything. Several times I reached the point where I felt that we had completely screwed up, that the damage was irreparable, that I could not help anything, do anything. At that point, usually, what happened was that I would look up and think, you just gotta give me this one.

Rick Shiomi

帰郷

帰郷

When the Japanese Canadian Centennial was coming up, we thought we would like to have a dance where everybody could join in the circle freely, and our idea was, how about doing these things on Powell Street?

I brought Rick Shiomi in because he lived on Cordova Street with other community workers. I knew that he was very capable. He also carries the spirit of the Japanese culture with him. He only needed a project.

Rick and I presented the proposal to the Centennial organizers in the fall of 1976, and we were treated like bugs. I was clearly told I was only an immigrant—the Centennial was not for immigrants, "not for you guys." I realized then how difficult the position of the Ijusha is in the Japanese Canadian community. Nikkei people think they've gone through a lot of trouble to have gotten this far, while Japanese like me, who have lived the easy life in Japan, come here and think they can do anything they want.

Takeo Yamashiro

There is a rootlessness to being Japanese Canadian. Going to high school, the Japanese Canadian kids never hung out together, never. But you would always see Chinese Canadian kids hanging out together, the Indo Canadian kids hanging out together. Japanese Canadians—we're white!

I'm aware of the statistics of intermarriage. I'm aware of how diverse we are. And in terms of our own psychology, I am a little taken aback by how Japanese Canadians shed the Japanese part of the hyphen. Any group can shed that part easily—Romanians, Hungarians, Chinese—but because of the influence of the war, I suspect, Japanese Canadians would really rather disappear altogether.

Ron Yamauchi

帰郷

太鼓
太鼓道

Being at the Powell Street Festival touches that which is essentially Japanese in me. It's the same feeling I get when I go to Japan. You're a stranger in lots of ways and you're recognizably so to them. Easily. But in your own heart, you don't feel that way, because there's something about the ambiance, the size of people, about the language which you know and have heard. All that has a kind of an echo in oneself, and the Powell Street Festival brings some of that out. One of the touching things about the Festival is how it's so deeply involved in perpetuating the mythology of the Japan most of us have lost. We hold it in our mind's eye as something desirable, that we treasure, but it's slipped through our fingers long ago in important ways. A lot of these things never even happen any more in Japan. That's what makes it poignant, that we hold onto these things out of that sense that without them who would we be?

Roy Kiyooka

I thought the Sansei were very energetic. They were trying to find out who they really were. They are Canadian-born but their faces are different from those of the majority. And yet, in the eyes of the Japanese people coming from Japan, they don't have the same Japanese culture we do. I sympathize with them. I wonder what I would do if I were in their shoes. I came from Japan and at least I have my identity.

That's why I feel sorry for the Sansei and I'm very interested in their search for their identity. My children will have to face the same problems one day. Since I am married to a Canadian, my children, apart from being Nisei or Sansei, were born from a mixed marriage and therefore, they are neither Japanese nor Caucasian. They may have something extra to consider.

Toshi Ito

There are these other people who are Japanese Japanese. I don't know what to make of them, because, to be quite honest, I don't like them. I don't like some of the ways they have or their attitudes. I don't like some of their philosophies around what's important and how they should be. I think it's very stifling.

Les Yamada

Festival in Japan, *matsuri*, is generally not co-ordinated by anybody. It just happens, there's no set schedule, it should have a craziness. The tradition goes back a really long time. You could do anything. Even if you want to sleep with someone, as long as you can sneak in without being noticed, you can do that. Nobody blames you. *Matsuri* was a time you can go wild. In Vancouver, *matsuri* is very well organized, very well mannered. I was disappointed a bit. Very orderly. Very quiet. You couldn't go beyond that square. Oppenheimer Park. I felt quite strange about it.

Shinobu Homma

Someone described our band as being weird. I didn't see anything weird. I sang a song about being a fish, being caught and deep-fried, and I sang a song about falling in love with a woman who'd been caught in a lava flow ten thousand years ago, and I thought those were pretty normal. When you think about Japanese culture, it's pretty weird anyway. There's that story about the forty-seven *ronin*—that's about the weirdest damn story I've ever heard in my life. It's beautiful and haunting and says everything about our culture. It says our culture is crazy and celebrates self-destructive honour over personal survival. From what little I understand of Japanese history, being staid and conservative in an *outward* way is all that there is.

Ron Yamauchi

A new immigrant and I had a big argument because I thought this should be a festival promoting Japanese Canadian culture, and he thought it was a chance to show what *matsuri* is, what Japanese culture is. But I didn't want Powell Street to be like the Sakura Festival in San Francisco—some pseudo-Japanese festival, an imitation of a Japanese festival.

I believed that Japanese Canadian people had their own history and culture. Even though some of them, whether they spoke Japanese or not, behaved even more Japanese than the Japanese—still I felt this was their way of life, not mine. I felt like I couldn't say "we." Because my "we" is Japanese, not necessarily the same as Japanese Canadian. When I had read about Japanese Canadian or Japanese American history in Japan, it was written in Japanese from a Japanese perspective, and always there was the assumption that "we are the same—in the bottom of their hearts, they are still Japanese." Even before I came here, I felt there was something wrong with this. They have 100 years of their own history, how can they be the same? Then when I met the Powell Street Festival people, I felt, "Yeah, they have their own way."

Not many Japanese businessmen come to the Powell Street Festival, because they feel that it is not authentic. And some Japanese immigrants feel the same way. They don't try to understand that we don't want to make a Japanese festival. It takes time to make them aware that they are part of a Japanese community here in Canada, because new immigrants don't share the history. Also they can go home. When the first Issei came, it was tough living here, but to go back to Japan was even tougher, so they stayed. Now, living here is pure choice, because they can probably make more money in Japan. So if they are going to stay here, they have to push themselves to understand why. Like the Sansei, new immigrants have to go through their own identity crisis.

And when Japanese Canadians have identity problems—they are not Japanese, they are not Canadian in the mainstream sense—I'd like the Festival to be able to show them what they are. Something like Katari Taiko, or the pompon dancers, or Roy Kiyooka. Through the Festival we can show people, we can tell people, "Relax, we can be what we are. This is all part of us. It's OK to be awkward compared to some mainstream image of Japanese Canadians. We can be different and it's OK to be different from Japanese Japanese."

Mami Miyata

I'm really tired of feeling like a banana. And it's finally occurred to me in the last few months, I suppose, that there's no such thing as a banana — you're not white on the inside, you're not yellow on the outside, you just are. I'm as representative of my generation of Japanese Canadians as anyone. I'm not a false- or half-Japanese, I'm not a false- or half-Canadian. I'm third-generation Japanese Canadian, and my idiosyncrasies come from my own personal psychology and background, and, dammit, I'm going to impose my way on people. That's why I wanted to do the Powell Street Festival—it's time for me to be Japanese in public. And I don't care to be half-white or half-yellow or a banana any more. I was never denying my heritage—I just simply never chose to make an issue of it. I make an issue of everything else.

The Festival is absolutely important for me. It's a reassurance that being Japanese Canadian is fun, that there's a prideful tradition here, that it's colourful, that it's a day when you can be Japanese Canadian and not be a lawyer, banker, clerk. It's just a time to be comfortable and to say that the traditions and heritage are worthy—worthy of respect and public display and celebration. I don't usually see myself as part of a sub-group minority culture. I'm just me—except at Powell Street. That day, a couple days ago, I was part of the Japanese Canadian community. I was singing to them, I was showing them my thoughts. And the rest of the year, I'm not going to be as Japanese Canadian as I am on Powell Street day. I think that's important. Whether or not it's good to be so limited or so discrete about it, I don't know.

I guess what I went down there to do was to see if I could be a Japanese Canadian artist. That's really important because what makes me passionate about going to Powell Street is that I think, "OK, we're part of a visible minority group, and we throw ourselves a party that allows us to be slack and to not try to be good at what we do. For once we don't have to do really great crafts and brilliant paintings and astonishing music. No, why should we? We're throwing ourselves a party, come one, come all."

Ron Yamauchi

帰郷

帰郷

お願い
食器を使用され
た後はかならず洗
って元の位置に戻し
て下さい。
SEL
18ℓ×1

After the first Festival, we said, "Wasn't it nice last year?" It was so successful and everyone felt good about it. It was only after the second one was over that people said, "Maybe we should do this every year." The second one in 1978 was all local performers—it was a very small festival. But that one was important—it gave us the confidence to know that we could do it, on a smaller scale, not as grandiose as the first one. It gave us continuity.

Mayu Takasaki

帰鄉

The first year I did a lot of construction. It was a wonderful feeling because there were so many people I'd never met before. There we were, trying to put these structures together, not being very efficient, but having a lot of fun. Suddenly the park was our park—we were all Asian, and we'd just taken it over! By building these physical structures, we were putting our own stamp on this park.

Ken Shikaze

We wanted to bring the focus back to the Powell Grounds, back to Powell Street. The Buddhist Church had moved its *obon* to Swangard Stadium, and there was this attitude that Powell Street was skid row. But there were still a lot of Issei and Nisei seniors who were living down there, and we didn't want their home to be considered skid row. Our dream was to regenerate Powell Street, to make it into a place where we could go, a place we would all identify with and become part of. The Festival was a key element in that dream that we could bring people back to this area where our roots are.

Rick Shiomi

The first years were the most exciting for me—working at Tonari Gumi with the seniors and putting on the Festival. The Issei were so enthusiastic. I think they were excited that Sansei were interested in going back into the community and reviving a community spirit. The Festival felt like a bridging, something the Sansei could do for the Issei. When the Issei planted the cherry trees in Oppenheimer Park that first year, it was like they were putting something of themselves into the ground. And the Festival emerged from it.

And just to see all the different generations over the years. No matter how you felt about redress, how you felt about the internment, how you felt about any of those issues—it was all put aside because there was a kind of longing for everyone to be all together to celebrate something.

Naomi Shikaze

hen I walk the grounds at Oppenheimer, I realize all these people are very similar to me but I don't know how to ask them what that means. I go every year, I need to go. But at the same time, being at the Festival teaches me a little bit more, and I don't know if I want to face it. I'm not sure if I'm going to say, "I'm going to embrace this now. This is me." I'm at the point where I don't know how much being Japanese is me and how much being Canadian is me. Whatever the hell that little mixture is in there. I've heard enough about what a lot of Nisei and Sansei are going through emotionally to understand what it is. For me, it feels like a different kind of journey, but I know I'm connected in there somewhere. I'm feeling more and more comfortable at the Festival, and I know I'm discovering a great part of myself with those people. But what holds me back is some sort of fear, taking a risk, fear of letting that cat out of the bag totally. Right now, it sort of has its head out of the bag, and it's looking around, checking it out. It wants to jump out. Part of me is still stuffing it down. But the bag is getting too small or the cat is getting too big.

Les Yamada

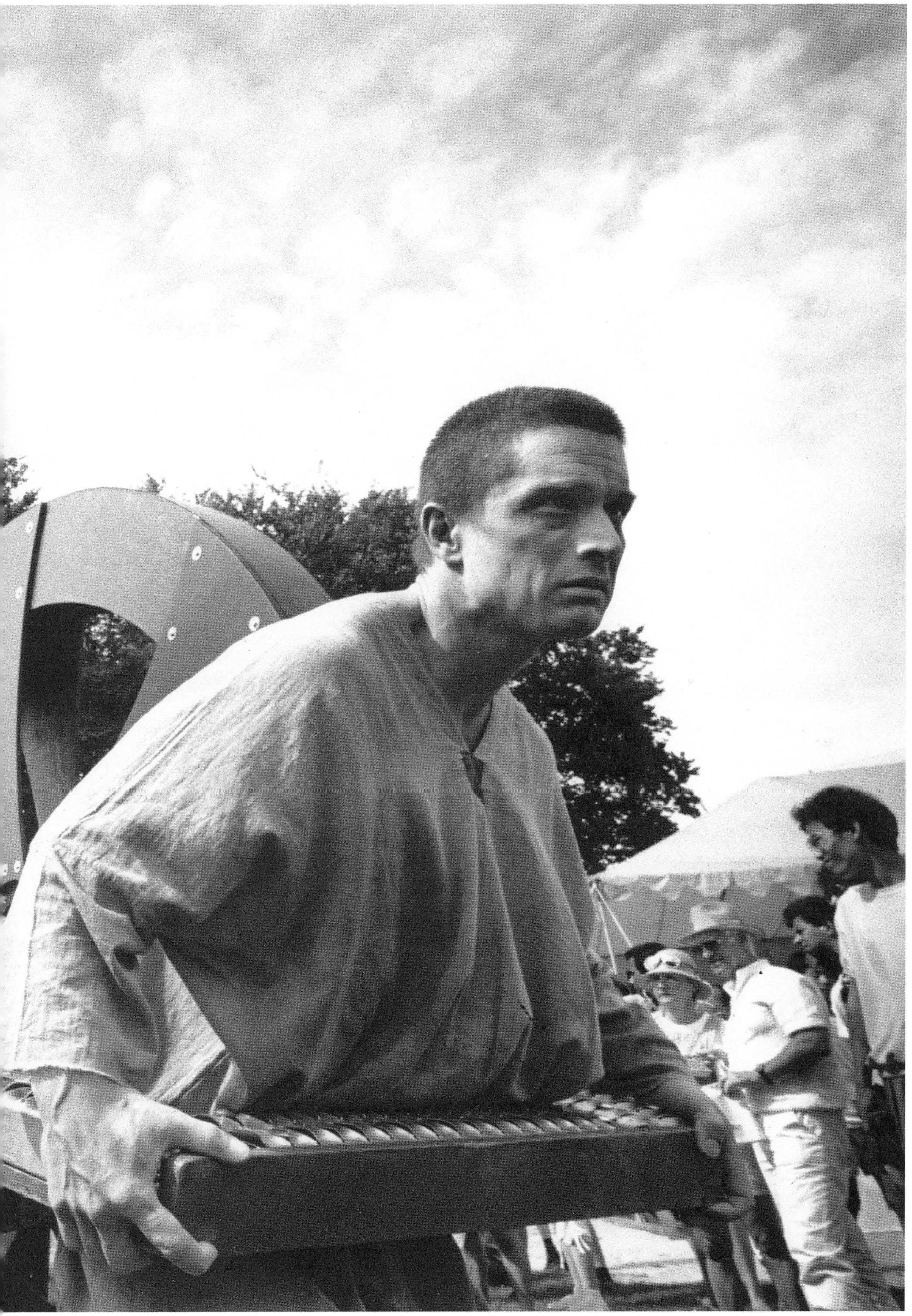

Struggling as an artist in the maelstrom of a dominant white culture, I realize how sadly disconnected I am from my ethnic background and the creative people in it. Occasionally, and only occasionally, do I have the pleasure to work with or amongst other Japanese Canadian artists. And always, I have found it to be a special encounter, and yes, for me at least, a connection of some undefinable understanding.

Powell Street Festival is a very special festival. It reveals the continuity of creative expression amongst its people. It is marvellous that there is a place for the contemporary to stand alongside the traditional. How rare this is, and how important! A culture must be seen and heard from every segment of every generation, the old and the new. Only in this manner can a heritage be established and carried forward, constantly enriched by new visions.

Bart Uchida

Two years ago, when we brought Bart Uchida for the second time, he did one of his installation pieces on the park grounds. I had a bit of free time and decided to go under the seniors' canopy to stand and watch with them. Part of Bart's piece was having Mami-san tell a folk tale in Japanese, and she proceeded to tell the story of Momotaro, the peach boy. So I can hear all the seniors going, "Oh, oh, this is the story of Momotaro. Oh, that's good." So they're watching, and actually what Mami is saying has nothing specifically to do with the piece, which was about the four walls, each wall representing a different generation. The seniors don't understand any of that. They only hear what Mami-san is saying in Japanese. And then Koko comes dragging herself in, all dressed in white with white make-up and clearly in distress. And I hear all around me, "That's not Momotaro. Where's Momotaro?" And suddenly the absurdity of it all hit me. But it was moving, in a sense. There they are thinking, "Oh, these crazy Sansei, what are they doing?" But there was some kind of bond nonetheless—it was the classic generation gap.

Mayu Takasaki

In 1990 I was most excited by Snake in the Grass Moving Theatre because their interpretation of Japanese culture was somehow more intense than a straight translation—it set up resonances within myself that were very powerful. I welcome that kind of piece in the Festival because it is legitimately Japanese Canadian culture, yet it's miles away from *ikebana* or *sumo*. That kind of performance is the future, however much the past has sentimental and nostalgic value. For me, the traditional arts are more stereotyped, and I don't relate to them in the same way.

Randy Enomoto

That first year the Festival had a strong Japanese colour. I still think that's better. There is something about cultural heritage. For instance, in *taiko* the process of changing Japanese culture, developing it—depth in the art cannot be achieved unless one keeps one's eye on the original source. Or it will become something totally different. I don't mean the different thing is wrong. But if you talk about Japanese Canadian culture, you must maintain the source, which is Japanese. For me as a Japanese Canadian *shakuhachi* player, I will get lost if I get cut off from my original source. The *taiko* of Katari Taiko and Uzume Taiko is different from that of Japan. It's not a question of good or bad. But if Canadian *taiko* only reproduces what jazz percussion instruments can do, then *taiko* becomes simply another instrument. Culture is more than an instrument. You must be conscious of the origin. So the Festival, too, must keep the door open to stimuli coming from the original source—Japan.

Takeo Yamashiro

The fact that the Festival operates on a shoestring, that it does not pay its performers and that people will nonetheless give their energy to that occasion, all that's really admirable. I deplore the professionalization of the arts where everything has to be doled out in appropriate little bits and you get paid for that and you get paid for this and one thing and another, and it becomes a kind of shell game. The real venues are where none of that's involved and people just say, "Hey, let's do it. Let's have some fun."

Roy Kiyooka

Powell Street Festival shows us Sansei in the arts, and the arts that aren't mainstream. You never see that anywhere else—the Sansei are usually so assimilated. It's good for them to see that there are other things out there. They don't have to stick to traditional assimilated roles—they don't have to just get an education and become an engineer or a chartered accountant or a lawyer.

Gordon Kayahara

帰郷

I always think Katari Taiko is a good example of Japanese Canadian culture. If I were asked if Katari Taiko is authentic, I'd say, "NO. You can find the root in Japanese traditional drumming. But the flower is different. The same seed put into Japanese earth or Canadian earth would grow differently." And that's how it should be.

The music is beautiful, but it moves me in my heart in a different way from how it moved me the first time—when their technique was so primitive and they were so shy. They moved my heart tremendously. They've changed from a community group, who just happened to fall in love with the sound of drums, into professional performers. I don't deny their growth and I'm very happy for them, but they don't move me as they did ten years ago. Still Katari Taiko is the best example of what I would like to achieve through the Festival—cultivating something ourselves.

Mami Miyata

What is being shown should transcend the trappings of the colour of your skin or the accent in your voice, especially with things that are visual, like the tea ceremony. A lot of that is the ceremony itself and the ritual of it and also the philosophy behind it. Things like *ikebana* and the tea ceremony take a lot of study and discipline and time, and it doesn't matter who is putting all this time and energy and thought into it. What comes out of it is what comes out of the discipline itself. You're a tea master—it doesn't really matter where you're from—because you have the spirit.

Les Murata

Some of the children are Nisei and Sansei, some are non-Japanese, but all of them are serious. The colours of their eyes are different, but human beings are all the same when they face serious situations. It has nothing to do with Nisei, Sansei or race. It has something to do with blood.

Hirotaka Ara

帰郷

Most of the other things I do, there are hardly any other Asians—I'm always in the minority. It's a horrible feeling—you feel marginalized in a way. You walk into a place and you're one of a very few. But this is an Asian festival. I've never been involved in the Chinese festivals, don't really even know about them. I feel pretty comfortable working here, just hanging out. Just being here with other Asians feels like a kind of brotherhood or sisterhood.

Anonymous

I feel good about non-Asians being involved in the Festival because it is an open festival. I think they feel it's an important event for our community, and they'd like to be part of it. I'm curious why more non-Japanese volunteer than from our own community. The Japanese Canadians don't look to their community or their background as viable or worthy to get involved in, whereas people from outside are finding it an enjoyable experience. I think the young Sanseis feel that the Festival is hokey, that because it is a community event, it's kind of amateurish and hokey.

Cathy Makihara

I think there are some parts of any community that have to maintain a certain integrity. This is a lousy analogy, but if you look at mongrel dogs, quite often they're better tempered, they're more intelligent, they have nicer personalities than purebreds who tend to be high-strung and irritable. So take a heterogeneous group—there should be pockets of integrity within that group, of homogeneity, that represent the purest form of whatever it is that community's all about.

Les Yamada

Why not have *hakujin* participants? Who among us has not married or had relatives who married *hakujin* or friends who are really keen about Japanese culture or language? I mean, how can you keep it pure? It's silly even trying to do it.... But I don't know about seeing a blonde up there doing *taiko*, you see, so...I don't know. But I just don't see how we can say no.

Midge Ayukawa

It does concern me that the volunteers at the Festival are not all Japanese Canadian. Audrey Kobayashi's statistics show, what, a ninety percent intermarriage rate amongst the Sansei? So if you accept that that's our community, then having non-Asian volunteers does reflect it. I don't have trouble with the outside volunteers —we couldn't survive without them. What I have trouble with is the lack of Sansei volunteers.

Gordon Kayahara

I think it's inevitable that *hakujin* would become more and more involved in the Festival. It's like the issue with Katari Taiko letting them into the group. I'm not a person who excludes. Look at how black music has been taken over by whites. I see that happening with Asian music too, as more and more *hakujin* are interested in the culture.

Kyoshi Shimizu

Powell Street's network is a community network. So even if people are not of Japanese descent, I regard them as part of this community, and we can't isolate ourselves from them. I don't believe in exclusivity of any kind. Monoculture doesn't really interest me, that's not where I live.

Diane Kadota

Maybe Sansei, Yonsei, Gosei in the future, those who intermarry, they might choose another culture, but why can't we say it's OK? Let the people blossom whoever they are. And it may be that the Powell Street Festival will be an anchor in place every year, so that these people might reflect and say, "Yes! This is what I should be choosing," or "Yes, I've seen it but I still choose something else." The Festival will be there to say, "Look at our history and our struggle. How wonderful it is."

David Murata

Eleven years ago when we first came to Vancouver for a holiday, I said to my girls, "Let's go to my old stamping grounds and I'll show you around." I took them down to Powell Street. Well, we were scared. I guess my children had been rather sheltered. They were in their early teens and they'd never seen drunks, they'd never seen toothless women wandering around and falling. All of this in the daytime. They were absolutely appalled. It was a scary place, not at all like what it used to be.

Midge Ayukawa

I was born on 654 Powell Street. I am really a local person. For Japanese, for the future, maybe it's not a very good location. One thing is—too many drunks. When you talk about Powell Street, the first thing they say is, "Oh, Skid Row." Nobody says, "Oh, Japanese town." And that's really bad for us.

I got fed up with the city. They don't care that much. Japanese people, we don't fight enough. We just yak, yak, yak like I do, but we're not strong enough. Chinatown is different, they have a good, strong community. They do it. If they want the liquor store to close, they'll close it. Japanese people, we're too quiet.

Shig Hirai

Every year there are people who come to us and say, "We should move the Festival," that it doesn't matter where it's held, that they don't like the environment, the rubby dubs, the native people, and suggest we move it God-knows-where.

When I was a kid, that park was no man's land, there wasn't a blade of grass growing there. There was a long period of about twenty years when it was a huge sandlot. Then, because of our Centennial year and the city's Neighbourhood Improvement Program, they upgraded the park. I think the Powell Street Festival was responsible for bringing life back to that park.

Some of my really good memories of the Festival have nothing to do with the actual Festival itself, but more with the residents of the park. They're there early Saturday morning as we're setting up, waiting with great expectations. "Hey, lady, are we going to do that coal miner's dance again?" Or "Looks like a good day this year." Or "You want some help, lady?" They're out there carrying tables and chairs. And I don't think they would ever hurt the Festival.

Mayu Takasaki

Given how small a community it is, the Festival is also extraordinarily diverse. The bulk of those people belong to a walk of life, a lifestyle that has nothing to do with the way I live my life. Japanese are exemplary middle class people, whether over there or here, they really are, and the adversarial part of myself has never had anything to do with that sensibility. It is the enemy in lots of ways, whatever colour it is, red or yellow or black or white. But I do like the collusion between us and the derelicts and the Indians on Powell Street. I like that intersection as a political place in which this kind of ritual is enacted. If the Festival became completely middle class I wouldn't go to it. Oh, the motley of people that show up. And to those who live in that immediate area, it's as important as it is to us. It gives them a social context into which they can disappear and enjoy themselves. I've seen that clearly on their faces.

Roy Kiyooka

When I first came to Vancouver from Montreal, I was so shocked by the homogeneity of the culture. It was so very bland—the dryest part of British and American culture. That was my original impression of Vancouver: a white wasteland. So I appreciated the mix of people at the Festival because the kids were raised in a pretty protected environment—a middle class environment—and I wanted them to be around people who looked different, so they wouldn't be scared by differences.

Renee Rodin

It's a really good festival, very well organized. It brings the park back up to the level of normal society, because otherwise this park is the end of the road. This is the downtown lower eastside, and a lot of people would look at it as being the lowest you could go in Vancouver. There's a lot of substance abuse that goes on here, but I think the people down here appreciate the Festival, so they don't get that blasted.

Mike Barrett

The 1990 Festival felt different. Other years when we were setting up, the people in the park minded their own business. This year, as soon as we got everything set up, they were hanging around, flipping the tables over. It's the first year that I noticed a slight edge to it. The parks people told us that the demographics are changing. So, while it's nice to hold the Festival down there because it is Powell Street, at the same time the Festival is for the community, and if you have senior Nisei and Issei and even Sansei feeling uncomfortable, then maybe it's not the best location.

But once the Powell Street Festival moves from Powell Street, it will have changed. Right now, the Festival is very much a grass roots festival, community-based. The Festival kind of holds the line on being Japanese Canadian. When it changes, it will move to a better area and become a middle class festival, I suspect. The programming will change. It will become a "very nice" program, probably more Japan-oriented. My feeling is that the Japanese Canadian community is on this road to assimilation. If the Powell Street Festival changes, it will be just one more event in our history to take us one step closer to assimilation.

Gordon Kayahara

帰郷

COMING HOME

Looking at the houses on Cordova Street with their badly slumped faces turned toward the proceedings, I tried to imagine the thriving community that existed before the war: the fishermen from Steveston who came into town to stay in the cheap hotels before partaking of Powell Street liquor, women and fighting; the *furoba* that concealed the gambling dens; the family stores that served the Issei picture brides and their children; the churches that housed the Word of God and the Teachings of Buddha; the mighty Asahi baseball team who performed their athletic choreography to the cheers of the gathered fans; the *New Canadian* office where the Nisei intellectuals gathered to discuss issues of racism and community. It was all there. The ghosts of Little Tokyo had encircled the Powell Street Festival to welcome back the Japanese Canadian community.

Terry Watada

VOLUNTEERS
INFORMATION

A lot of people left during internment and said, "I'm not going back to the coast. They kicked us out and I'm never going back." And people still have that idea. I know some friends of mine do. But the strange thing is, as they get into their senior years, they want to come back. It's like the salmon going back to the river.

Dick Nakamura

The Powell Street Festival, to me, was a celebration of something that up until then had been kept silent in my generation—we did not celebrate ourselves. And I think that was the political consequence of my parents' generation. The silence coming, literally, from their removal from the coast. And the shame coming from their feeling that although they weren't responsible for that action, the removal was not something you could be proud about. The continuing silence was a residue of that shame. And we Sansei wanted to come out of that silence and give voice.

Randy Enomoto

サンノゼ
太

帰郷

INVITATIONAL
GOLF TOURNAMENT

帰郷

Immigrants had a lot of experience being in festivals in Japan, which is a very rich and very happy occasion in your life. Because everybody's happy—people get dressed up, people give money, they decorate, make the town beautiful, go out in the streets at night. All the immigrants have that experience and always miss it, living in North America. And then the second and third generations realized it also: that feeling of *matsuri* is a wonderful feeling. Everybody wants to share and nourish it, so more people get involved.

Many Japanese Canadians didn't want to get involved in something so obviously Japanese as a Japanese festival, because they were always being made to feel bad about being Japanese. But the Festival didn't make them feel bad—it made them feel good about being Japanese. It's like a spirit that nourishes the people. You may know mentally or intellectually what Japanese is, but what's the feeling ?

Now we have kids who are fourteen, fifteen, sixteen, who have been brought up with the Festival, from the time they were born, when they were being carried by Mother. They crawled in the grass of the Festival. So they know the feeling. And suddenly, when we were in Japan in August, my son Kaya says to me, "I wish I were at the Powell Street Festival."

Michiko Sakata

The festival is *kyodo genso*. It's a shared fantasy or illusion. Very difficult to translate. Being able to be yourself and, from the bottom of your being, to relate to each other—everybody, at the same time—and then create something.

Shinobu Homma

I used to live on Cordova Street and I'd look out on Oppenheimer Park and think, "I wonder what it'd be like to be involved in the Japanese Canadian community? I wonder who these people are?" I'd grown up and worked in a mixed, mainstream Canadian environment. In the previous four or five years I'd been living in, basically, a counterculture milieu. I'd explored all these different areas but there was this one huge area called Japanese Canadian which I hadn't really touched. So I thought, "Well, I'll take a look at this." Of course, to my huge surprise, that's where everything was.

Rick Shiomi

帰郷

You bump into your old friends either at a funeral or at the Powell Street Festival.

Shirley Kakutani

If the Powell Street Festival didn't continue, it would be like a lost love affair for me. What is there left in a love affair down through the years? Just a few very special moments that you hang onto.

Roy Kiyooka

AFTERWORD

PAUL WONG

Park

Oppenheimer Park is a city block in the downtown eastside of Vancouver. At one end is a baseball diamond, a drinking fountain and a clubhouse with toilets and change rooms. At the other end is a small playground, a basketball court and a knoll of grass with half a dozen cherry trees. These trees were planted by Japanese Canadian seniors in 1977 as a centennial project to commemorate the first Japanese immigrant to Canada. A row of old big trees and wooden benches edges the park. The benches are mostly used by drunks, old-age pensioners and street people. There is no sign announcing the name of the park (Oppenheimer was a former mayor). Although there are signs forbidding public drinking and restricting use of the park from 10 p.m-6 a.m., the park has no fences to keep it from being used at all hours.

Powell Street runs along the north side, where it routes traffic into downtown. The street is made up of half-empty storefronts, a bar, a coffee shop and a couple of Chinese and Japanese food shops. To the south is Cordova Street, a traffic route from downtown. Several newer housing units, a public health centre and a funeral home face the mountains. On the west side is the Franciscan Sisters of the Atonement Mission, one of the oldest and largest church agencies in the area. Its late afternoon breadline stretches down the sidewalk. Sharing this block is the New World Hotel in the Tamura Building, named after the Japanese businessman who built the four-storey brick hotel in 1912. Across from the hotel is a Buddhist church rebuilt in bland, mid-1970s, low-cost style. Next to that are four identical turn-of-the-century wooden houses in need of repairs.

The park is for mixed use, but in reality it is a green space of despair. Real or imagined violence is ever present. Not once, but twice a friend has stumbled upon boxes of bullets. Although prostitution and heroin have been part of the neighbourhood for decades, the fear of AIDS is producing more visible evidence of these activities: used condoms and syringes are not uncommon litter.

This is "skid road"—a few neglected blocks of cheap hotels, light manufacturing, storage warehouses, rooming houses, secondhand stores, breadlines, social housing, artists' studios, strip bars and Japanese shops. The City of Vancouver police headquarters, courthouse and jail are one block west. Gastown, a typical brick, brass and fern tourist zone, is one block west of that. The Canadian National Railroad and the harbour are two blocks north of the park. The business centre of Chinatown and the active, working-class Strathcona neighbourhood are one block to the south.

Before World War Two, this was Little Tokyo, a major residential and business area. But in 1942, the federal government forcibly removed 22,000 Japanese Canadians from the West Coast and barred them from returning until 1949. An ethnic minority was dispersed, assimilated and almost disappeared, and Powell Street never recovered.

For two days a year, the Powell Street Festival reclaims this park and the surrounding streets as a public site for the reunion and renewal of a displaced community. The loss of face, the denial of self and of home are so deeply rooted that the process of re-creating a sense of community is difficult. The annual Festival is home to a diminished spirit and provides a context for exploring this loss of identity. 1992 is a significant year for Japanese Canadians and Americans. It is fifty years since internment, fifteen years since the annual Powell Street Festival began and almost five years since both governments announced official redress and apology for the injustices of the war years.

Camp

After Japan bombed Pearl Harbor in a surprise attack on December 7, 1941, there was widespread fear that an invasion of

West Coast shores was imminent and that Japanese Canadians would act as a fifth column and assist in the invasion effort. All people of Japanese origin were considered a risk to national security. Everyone over sixteen was fingerprinted and issued photo identification, which they had to carry until 1949. Dusk-to-dawn curfews were strictly enforced, and all means of communication and transportation were confiscated: radios, cameras, cars, trucks, farm rigs, bikes, fishing vessels and anything else that floated.

Hastily erected batteries dotted the coastline to alleviate public hysteria. Plans were swiftly put together to remove all people of Japanese descent from the West Coast. Many single and married men were separated from their families and sent to road camps. Rebellious men—some community leaders and those who tried to avoid the road camps—were either jailed or sent to higher security camps. Women, children and other men were interned in makeshift camps in remote areas of BC and farms across the country. Most lived in crude substandard conditions for almost four years. Life continued in the camps: infants learned to walk, children reached puberty, couples fell in love. People also died, some from natural causes, others from lack of proper medical facilities, a few from suicide.

Meanwhile the Custodian of Enemy Alien Property seized all remaining property, telling the owners it was for safekeeping: homes, businesses, cars, boats, real estate, livestock and personal effects. These were later auctioned off for a fraction of what they were worth, or taken by neighbours and never returned. The explanation was that revenue from the sale of goods would help pay for their incarceration.

It comes as no surprise to Asian Canadians that this could occur. White Canada has always felt threatened by Asian immigration, except when it needed cheap expendable labour. Every possible means has been used to prevent Asians from coming to Canada: legislated head tax, exclusion acts, racial quotas, labour laws, restrictions on the right to vote. In 1942, amid war hysteria and the effects of the great Depression, Canada did not need much of an excuse to dispossess Japanese Canadians. Government officials at all levels approved racism and tolerated Jap-hating.

Tamio Wakayama was born in 1941 and was one of the youngest to be interned, first in the cattle stalls of Hastings Park and then at Tashme, BC. He grew up branded an "enemy alien". This is the cruel reality that has informed and shaped his psyche.

Chinese

Because I grew up in the fifties and the sixties, I have only recently understood my own resistance to the Japanese. Perhaps I was influenced by the horrific stories my mother told me about the Japanese occupation of China. She immigrated to Prince Rupert, BC in 1949, the same year that the Japanese Canadians were allowed to return west of the Rockies. I believe she distanced herself from them as a survival technique—to avoid being mistaken for Japanese. During the war, many merchants displayed signs declaring themselves to be Chinese.

Growing up I was often asked if I was Chinese or Japanese. I can now fully appreciate having the surname Wong and not Wakayama. The term "all you Asians look alike" is a common excuse used by bureaucrats and law enforcement officers to detain us or ignore us. Funny how on the street, racist bullies can quickly distinguish what you are, spewing out "chink" to a Chinaman or "nip" to a Jap. This is usually done loudly if they are in groups, if not quietly in a threatening manner so only you can hear.

One of the many Chinese Canadian volunteers at the Powell Street Festival is a voice in *Kikyō*: "Most of the other things I do, there are hardly any other Asians—I'm always in the minority. It's a horrible feeling—you feel marginalized in a way.... But this is an Asian festival. I've never been involved in the Chinese festivals, don't really even know about them. I feel pretty comfortable working here, just hanging out. Just being here with other Asians feels like a kind of brotherhood or sisterhood."

This person was the only one who insisted on anonymity. We considered not including the statement, or signing it with an alias, but in the end, this anonymous voice represented a far too common attitude within the Asian community. After generations of repression, opposing voices have been silenced. Asians have learned to be as invisible as possible: middle-of-the-road; mediocrity as a way of life.

Racism

Racist stereotypes of Asians are in perpetual motion: one decade we are buck-toothed, subservient coolies, the next we are greedy and sinister gooks; evil kung fu killers or fanatical soldiers; high-tech capitalist consumers or drug warlords. Asians continue to be visible objects of hatred. The damage done to Japanese Canadians cannot be repaired or excused simply with a forced apology and minimal financial compensation. It is not enough to pretend that racism doesn't exist by declaring that you are personally not racist.

In the newest wave of anti-Asian sentiment, the current economic woes of the United States and Canada are being blamed on Japan. Japan-bashing is an easy out for government and corporate leaders, who are actually responsible for our economic problems. Not so long ago, "made in Japan" meant cheap and inferior goods; now the slogan "Buy North American" specifically implicates Japan and Asian countries. Both strategies were created to confuse the consumer. The emergence of Japan as a major economic power is a direct result of postwar American foreign policy.

In BC, the escalating price of real estate—out of reach of the common worker—is conveniently blamed on the influx of rich Hong Kong immigrants and offshore buying. Offshore implies Asians. The invisible majority such as Germans, Americans and other Canadians have not been blamed. Government- and business-created hatred of Asians in general becomes aggression against individuals: recent documented violence against Asians is on the rise. In Detroit, for example, Asians driving Japanese-made cars have been visible targets.

Meanwhile, there is continuing resistance to anti-racist education programs in the workplace and in government and academic institutions. This is partly because many whites are not willing to accept the notion that widespread racism does exist. Admitting that there is a problem would mean having to take responsibility to make radical change, and to surrender privilege. Privilege is based on maintaining power and wealth.

Community/Art

More and more white artists are being accused of cultural and artistic "appropriation." The history of western art is littered with examples of symbols, styles and forms stolen from other cultures. Taken without giving credit to its origins, incorporated without understanding its intended cultural significance, this material has been plundered and used to misrepresent the cultures in which it originated. Whites with privileged access to the marketplace retell others' stories, they present and reshape them in their own view. Meanwhile, the originators are not given opportunities to tell their own stories, not given support to make their own books or create their own art. The representation of who or what we are has always been by and for the eurocentric standards of taste and acceptability.

Music is perhaps the clearest example of appropriation. Musical trends popularized by white musicians are credited as new and innovative. Blues and rock'n'roll are rooted in Black American culture, yet it is mostly white composers who have become the mega-stars of these forms. World Beat is a buzzword for "look at what I appropriated from the third world." The African Beat, a hybrid contemporary form popular in parts of Africa, is re-presented as an "international form" by non-Africans throughout the first world. Few Africans have been signed on by major record labels in North America or Europe. Appropriators argue that if it wasn't for them, these forms would remain unappreciated and unknown. Unknown to and unappreciated by whom?

I have attended numerous panel discussions, workshops, conferences and lectures centred on issues of race and cultural practice. Often, these talks are about the lack of accessibility by visible minorities to a eurocentric standardized art world, and how this elite continues to silence other voices. More often than not, bolting aggressively out of their chairs, whites dominate the discussion. Meanwhile, the new and intended minority audience dares not speak out. Thinking out loud, speaking, shouting, debating postmodernism—neocolonialism is couched in white theory and artspeak. Constructive dialogue is often destroyed by their need to be heard and understood.

When visible minority artists reference ethnicity in their work, it is almost always perceived as amateur/community-based art limited to special interest groups. Arts education, criticism and funding are tailored to acceptable European "standards of quality." Aware of growing pressure but closed to "other" sensibilities, programmers and funders are scrambling to provide token inclusion. Every institution is trying to "do the right thing" for the same conservative white audience. Decisions and validation are still based on the same old "A list."

True avant-garde or oppositional art cannot coexist within the established "fine art" framework of galleries and museums that are largely concerned with art as a financial investment or historical artifact. "Acceptable" fine art serves only the limited vision of an artist producing for a narrow marketplace, and an established few who control the access and consumption of art, and who maintain the status quo. Many of the demands and gains made by innovative artists have been compromised and co-opted by conservatives and academics.

The Powell Street Festival provides a forum for cultural investigation and expression outside the monolithic ideology, a support structure that encourages a community to look at itself. Self-reflection is not necessarily narcissism. When the Festival began, Japanese Canadians no longer wanted to fit invisibly into the dominant culture. Finding out exactly what and who they can be required exploration into the unknown. The new world—the land of opportunity—is finally being questioned, and the concept of equality is being redefined on different terms.

The Festival has accomplished what many anti-mainstream communities, artists and organizations are just starting out or hoping to do. It has created an inclusive venue, a collective experience that successfully programs ethnic folk art alongside contemporary art, popular culture with high art, static with performing arts. The Festival is an environment that includes the participation of community, neigbourhood and cross-cultural audiences, and maintains social and political integrity. Developing in isolation, the Powell Street Festival has created a unique "space."

Like the Festival, the photos in *Kikyo* are a diverse, inclusive collection: traditional folk dancing, crafts and martial arts comfortably juxtaposed with rock music, concrete poetry and experimental performance art. Throughout the book there are images of Katari Taiko, a Japanese drumming group that perhaps best exemplifies the new hybrid Japanese Canadian culture. It embodies a spirit of renewal and is a metaphor for the growth of the Festival itself.

Taiko (drumming) is a traditional form, historically a performing group of a dozen or so men. The first Powell Street Festival featured a group from Japan, the third Festival a group from San Jose, and following that, a group of Festival volunteers formed Katari Taiko. KT is an ideal medium to fuse North American backgrounds with Asian heritage and a perfect vehicle for bridging generation, language and gender barriers. A Katari Taiko performance is a visceral experience, a thunder of intense drumming and visual assault of precision performers. It is a cacophony of rhythms built upon layers of complicated musical scores that have been learned orally and combined with sharp choreography, yelling, theatrics and other percussive sounds. The group is a collective of nine women and three men, committed to social, political and environmental concerns, who perform at various venues throughout the year. KT's present members are all of Asian descent and the group gives priority to Asian Canadians when choosing new members. Membership over the years has included whites, and the current policy has evolved over years of hard discussion and debate within the group.

Like the Powell Street Festival itself, Katari Taiko is reaching middle age. As well as being physically demanding, the work requires extensive rehearsal time, and all members support themselves with daytime jobs. Three key members left Katari Taiko in 1989 to form Uzume Taiko, mainly to go professional, and once again the *taiko* form is being radically transformed. A three-member unit will create a very different sound and look than a larger group.

Photography/Documentary

Tamio Wakayama's approach to photography is grounded in the traditions of photojournalism and the firsthand experience he gained as part of the civil rights movement in the American South from 1963 to 1965, the most profound period of discovery in his life. Working with the Student Nonviolent Coordinating Committee and then as part of the Southern Documentary Project, he became a a political activist and visual communicator.

In the early sixties, when Wakayama went South, the television medium was still in its infancy. The family b/w Zenith TV set picked up the crude VHF signal with "rabbit ears" or, if you were lucky enough, from a rooftop antenna that got a slightly stronger signal. Selection was limited to two or three channels. *The Tonight Show*, *I Love Lucy*, Ed Sullivan and Walter Cronkite were your viewing staples. In Canada, the CBC weekly *This Hour Has Seven Days* was considered hot television journalism. Television technology was cumbersome, and news pictures depended on the delayed use of film footage.

America was still enjoying the international power and prestige it acquired after winning World War Two, and after the fifties—a decade of making babies, making money, making technology, making movies and making politics—mass media was becoming a part of everyday life. People looked to television for entertainment and live broadcasting of sporting events, but they looked to the daily papers and radio for up-to-the-moment news. Picture weeklies such as *Life* magazine were an important source of information. In 1925, Leitz had produced the first 35-mm film camera, which used 35-mm movie film and revolutionalized photojournalism, and the picture weeklies were quick to make use of the powerful and spontaneous photographs that small, hand-held cameras could capture. Documentary photography equated authenticity with truth and therefore had enormous impact. New printing technologies allowed the photo-essay form to reach millions of people, and readers' appetite for dramatic pictures was insatiable: war reportage, ethnographic pictorials, social landscapes, political events and depictions of America's industrial accomplishments.

Wakayama grew up in the formative years of mass media, the golden age of television and Marshall McLuhan's theoretical construct of the "Global Village." The relative calm of the fifties had not prepared the American people for the television revolution of the sixties, beaming the political turmoil on the streets and the war in Vietnam into their homes. The "almost live" assassination of John F. Kennedy in 1963 launched television's magnetic decade, revealing its enormous influence and persuasive powers.

Improvement on the human condition has not kept up with advances in the electronic revolution. The small video camcorder is again radically altering our perceptions of reality. It is collapsing the boundaries between professional and amateur television. But what we see, we don't necessarily get to believe, as in a recent incident in Los Angeles. The videotape of a group of white police officers brutally beating a single black man, Rodney King, was the central piece of evidence in a court case charging the officers with using excessive force. The outcome, in favour of the police, denied reality. It is seen by many, not just the black community, as an open act of racism, and it is triggering a violent reaction against white authority.

In his introduction, Wakayama states: "I turned on the TV to witness a spectacle unfolding at a small, segregated diner in Danville, Virginia. With raw eggs and Coke streaming down their faces, black youth sat calmly at the forbidden lunch counter in a maelstrom of racial hate and violence. From the deep but yet unnamed echoes of my own past came the compelling need to go South." Up to then, his perception of mass media, both fiction and nonfiction, had only negative connotations. Mass culture had equated Japanese with evil and inferior.

Civil rights movement workers understood the power of media. When Wakayama walked into a historical moment, working with the Student Nonviolent Coordinating Committee, he not only learned the fundamentals of political activism, he learned how social change can be effected through photographs. In this environment, photography was not just a tool to

record history in the making, but was authentic visual proof that could provoke further grassroots activism and, more important, could encourage Blacks to register to vote. The presence of photojournalists at voter registration campaigns provided both moral support and protection from violent attacks. It was a volatile time. Where, when, what to photograph and how to take a good frame required skill: an acute understanding of the context, intuition, sensitivity, a sharp eye, and quick reflexes.

Wakayama's trial by fire during the Civil Rights Movement directly informed his work photographing the Powell Street Festival. Here Wakayama is not an objective journalist on assignment, but a key player in a complicated fractured community undergoing critical transformations. This is a work of nonfiction based on more than 10,000 photographs taken over a fifteen-year period. Wakayama uses 35-mm Nikons loaded with 400 ASA film, shooting mostly through a 20-mm wide-angle lens and using available light. This is straight photography in the purest sense. The images have not been altered, multilayered or overly reworked in the darkroom.

The camera is an extension of his mind's eye, the photograph the evidence; we are witnesses to Wakayama's time of discovery. All of the pictures were taken spontaneously, none of the subjects formally posed. The only exception appears on page 70, a group picture of Festival volunteers taken in 1978. Throughout, there appears a relaxed and open relationship between the subject and the photographer. Although this project is based on the loss of a communal identity and the struggle to locate the self, the subjects here are not depicted as victims, but rather caught in moments of excitement, off guard, in performance or dancing or eating. These images tell the truth, defying stereotyped images of the assimilated Japanese and giving lie to the monolithic perceptions of multiculturalism, be it the Canadian "mosaic" or the American "melting pot."

Except in the first few pages, the photos and text are not necessarily shown chronologically or organized in obvious thematic order. This deliberate narrative strategy frees the individual pictures and voices from having to present a linear or literal historical record. Ambiguity is introduced to allow photographs to play with text, to allow associations that are sometimes complementary and sometimes contradictory. Composition, shape, light and subject relationships occur unexpectedly. Some sections are formal and minimal, others dense and cluttered. The rhythms are created by single images and no picture or text appears more than once. Similarity/familiarity is continuity, starkness can be for punctuation or pause for contemplation. The photographs are not captioned or dated except briefly in the photo index (page 161). The year in which each photograph was taken is not important to reading them. The book is a summation of a community's experience.

Visual signifiers of clothing and hairstyles normally help to situate a photograph in linear time, but the Festival attracts a truly diverse and eclectic crowd. Older people wear the same styles for decades, poorer people are not so obsessed with up-to-date fashions, street people wear it all. This is an outdoor summer event: shorts, T-shirts, bohemian casual merge with traditional *kimonos* and martial arts uniforms. The only noticeable changes are the stage sets and the size of the cherry trees planted in 1977.

Myth/Truth

Images of Natives appear throughout *Kikyō*, because many Native people live in the Powell Street neighbourhood and participate in the Festival. They are mostly poor and disenfranchised Natives. Careful consideration was given to how Natives are presented. By including certain images, is the artist reinforcing negative racial stereotypes? Is he being "politically incorrect"? The whole notion of "positive image-making" of visible minorities has been motivated by liberal do-good guilt. Corporations and all levels of government have funds and policies that support "positive projects," a strategy that easily erases reality. The image of the yuppie Indian (the "good" Indian) does not represent the norm. It is a fictional construct of "success" that fits into the colonial fantasy of assimilated values. The "skid road" Indian is a reality, the uneducated Indian is a reality, the drunk Indian is reality, abused women, broken men and hungry children are the victims of an imposed reality.

Wakayama presents the reality of downtown eastside Natives. This is a park they know, this is a festival they attend. This is home, where some dance, sing and openly make their presence felt. Look at the images carefully: the Natives depicted in these pages are active participants, no better and no worse than anyone else.

Without a doubt, this collection of photographs and testimonials will be as controversial within the Japanese Canadian community as outside of it. The messages here are mixed; it is a complex narrative full of contradictions and biases. This is a vision that has come out of self-hate, from resentment of past injustices to a proud, active challenge of mainstream perceptions. Documentary photography can only provide a controlled, limited view of the subject. The act of framing, shooting and editorially placing an image instantly distorts its authenticity. These images, covering a fifteen-year period and juxtaposed with excerpted texts, only re-create "history." On the other hand, this is most likely the closest you'll get to a truth.

Wakayama is fully aware of his artistic intent. "My images are indeed myth," he writes, "but the importance of myth lies not in its correspondence with reality, but rather with its creation of vision, the proverbial light to lead us to the end of a dark tunnel." He has described himself as the "informal historian of the contemporary Japanese Canadian community, the person who visually documents the life of the community and a particular aspect of it." I see Wakayama not as mythmaker, nor as historian. He is very close to the truth, and through the production of this work of art, his vision transcends the burden of recording history in so-called scientific terms. Great art reflects the society it is from, revealing its ugly truths as well as its glorious achievements.

Kikyō

Race and representation are among the most critical issues of this decade. At a time when the whole country is preoccupied with how national unity can coexist with distinct cultures, the Powell Street Festival, a fifteen-year process of discovery, makes a significant contribution to identifying the problems inherent in a multicultural society. It is a microcosm of all the questions plaguing the post-colonial world. *Kikyō*, a photodocumentary of a unique event, is a rare record of how a diminishing visible minority has struggled with self-determination. This struggle has strong implications for other cultural groups: among other things, it is a significant step toward rectifying aboriginal injustices.

In 1977, when the first Powell Street Festival was held, official bilingualism was still a new and idealistic concept, and multiculturalism barely a buzzword. Twenty-five years later, the political and cultural climate of North America is indeed shifting, and bilingualism may be on the verge of collapse. Quebec is demanding to be recognized as a distinct society with extraordinary provincial powers. Native leaders are demanding aboriginal rights, settlement of land claims and self-government. The one-sided utopian vision of multicultural harmony is being debunked.

Kikyō represents the longing for home. The meaning of home in the new world has always been transitional: leaving the old country to create Little Tokyos, Little Italys and Chinatowns is temporal. This land of opportunity beckoned the disenfranchised escaping from economic strife, political upheaval and religious persecution. Most came as unskilled labourers from modest agricultural villages into the age of mechanical reproduction. The classic immigrant story is one of selflessness, working hard to provide offspring with formal education that would allow them to attain prosperity, respectability and the civilities of home.

Wakayama writes, "Today the Nikkei are an endangered species. Our present high rate of intermarriage is not only a striking anomaly in comparison with other ethnic groups but also, taken to its logical conclusion, it will render meaningless the very concept of Japanese Canadians as a distinct and definable community." Striving to disappear into the dominant culture has been epidemic within the Nikkei community. Not surprisingly, ninety percent of Japanese Canadians born during and after World War Two have married *hakujin* (whites).

Moving on up means moving out of the ethnic ghetto. Aspiring to and assimilating into dominant middle-class values is a sure sign of success. Like it or not, all the trappings of the suburban lifestyle and shopping mall culture *is* the dream of riches. That it can be attained in only one lifetime of hard work continues to reverberate throughout the ancestral villages of faraway homelands.

If home is a place that one can call one's own, if home is a place of refuge, a safe haven with a nurturing family, then home is not Powell Street. Until World War Two, Powell Street represented optimistic beginnings. Now it seems to reflect only the failures—the end of the road, a few undesirable blocks of social agencies, bottom-end shops and restaurants. If home is transitory and a natural progression, for Japanese Canadians it has also meant the unconditional surrender of home during the war years. Relocation has a way of invoking a sense of loss, nurturing the mythology of home based on a faint memory of what it was, or what it must have been. In this context, "coming home" is an abstraction.

Perhaps due to the insidious destruction of their visible community home, Japanese Canadians have been forced to achieve invisibility far faster than other ethnic minorities. If achieving full assimilation is a desirable goal, then they have succeeded. "I am Canadian" usually refers to a third- or fourth-generation person who has no visible link to another homeland, a homogeneous identity without ethnic heritage—blandly Canadian. *Kikyō: Coming Home to Powell Street* is an attempt to stop, to examine and locate this accelerated loss of identity. These images and words re-create an ideological moment of reclaiming and making history: fragments of memory that provide clues to an "other" self.

GLOSSARY

ebi	shrimp, prawn
furoba	bathhouse
Gosei	fifth generation
hakujin	Caucasian
Ijusha	immigrants (refers here to postwar immigrants from Japan)
ikebana	art of flower arrangement
Issei	first generation (immigrants from Japan)
kyodo genso	shared fantasy or illusion; a term coined by Japanese philosopher Ryumei Yoshimoto in his book *Kyodo Gensoron*
matsuri	festival
mochi	rice cake
Nikkei	of Japanese descent (refers here to Japanese Canadians)
Nisei	second generation
obāchan	grandmother (familiar form)
obon	Buddhist summer festival celebrating the return of ancestral spirits
omikoshi	portable shrine carried at festivals
ozoni	a soup with mochi and vegetables, traditionally eaten at New Year's
ronin	a masterless samurai
Sansei	third generation
sumo	Japanese wrestling
taiko	Japanese drum, drumming
Yonsei	fourth generation

THE PHOTOGRAPHS

15	Harold Hirose (Japanese Canadian Cultural Centre), Powell Street, Vancouver, BC, c. 1912
17	Japanese Canadian Cultural Centre, Powell Street Parade
20	Omikoshi, 1990
22	Site construction, 1977
23	Masayo Hora, site construction, 1977
24	Sumo wrestlers, 1977
25	Site construction, 1977
26	Site construction, 1977
28	Tonari Gumi seniors planting cherry trees, 1977
29	Odori (public folk dancing), 1977
30	Odori , 1977
31	Odori , 1977
32	Spectators, 1980
33	Odori , 1978
34	Odori , 1977
35	Spectators, 1980
36	Kazuko Hohki of Frank Chickens, 1991
38	Katari Taiko, 1983
39	Katari Taiko, 1983
40	John Endo Greenaway of Katari Taiko, 1981
41	Ayako Morimoto of Mutsumi Kai, 1986
42	Seito ha Shorinji Kempo Sekai Rengo, 1983
43	Catarina ("Cat") Santos of San Francisco Taiko Dojo, 1980
44	Teresa Kobayashi, koto & Takeo Yamashiro, shakuhachi, 1980
47	Linda Uyehara Hoffman of Katari Taiko, 1981
48	Odori , 1981
49	Nishikawa Kayo of Nishikawa Ryu, 1987
50	Hiroko Tamano of Ankoku Buto, 1980
51	Daniel le Batteleur, 1986
52	San Francisco Taiko Dojo, 1980
53	Mrs. Eiko Morishita of the Tonari Gumi Seniors' Dance Group, 1990
54	Jan Woo of Katari Taiko, 1987
57	Renbu Dojo food booth, 1991
58	Yukio Moizumi, Tonari Gumi food booth, 1987
59	Renbu Dojo food booth, 1987
60	Tonari Gumi food booth, 1984
61	Tonari Gumi kitchen, 1990
62	Ruth Huang Suzuki of Sakura Singers, 1988
63	Ron Yamauchi of The Madding Crowd, 1991
64	Sumo spectators, 1989
65	Site construction, 1988
66	Bart Uchida, 1988
67	Site construction, 1988
68	Site construction, 1977
69	Seniors' tent, 1987
70	Volunteers, 1978
72	"Ghosts in the Machine," Snake in the Grass Moving Theatre, 1990
74	Paul Gibbons in Bart Uchida's sculptural/installation piece, "Four Notations," 1988
75	Spectators, 1980
76	"Four Notations," 1988
77	Bart Uchida's sculptural/installation piece, 1985
78	"Ghosts in the Machine," 1990
79	Hiroko Tamano of Ankoku Buto, 1980
80	"Ghosts in the Machine," 1990
81	Roy Kiyooka, 1988
82	Koto Ensemble of Greater Vancouver, 1980
83	Terry Watada, 1988
84	Rise Inokido of Kozakura Ryu, 1984
85	"Ghosts in the Machine," 1990
86	Zorra Mock in "Ghosts in the Machine," 1990
87	Jan Woo of Katari Taiko, 1990

THE CONTRIBUTORS

Hirotaka Ara (Ijusha, born in Fukushima, Japan, 1942) is a retired steelworker who directs the Burnaby Renbu Dojo. This kendo group has been involved with the Powell Street Festival since the first year as martial arts participants and, in recent years, has also operated a food booth.

Michiko (Midge) Ayukawa (Nisei, born in Vancouver, BC, 1930) was interned in Lemon Creek, BC during World War Two. Following the war her family moved to Ontario. She eventually settled in Ottawa but in 1980 moved to Sooke, BC. She has a B.Sc and M.Sc in chemistry, a B.A. and M.A. in history, and is currently working on her Ph.D. in history on Japanese pioneers in Canada.

Mike Barrett has worked at Oppenheimer Park for the past two summers as a staff member of the Carnegie Centre. He is a science student at Vancouver Community College, Langara Campus.

Randy Enomoto (Sansei, born in Bralorne, BC, 1944) is a training coordinator for the BC Ministry of Social Services. Since his involvement with the Japanese Canadian Centennial Project, which produced the book and photo exhibit *A Dream of Riches* in 1977, he has been very active in the Japanese Canadian community. He was instrumental in establishing redress as an open issue for the community when he was elected to the JCCA Board of Directors in 1984. He has served on the JCCA Board for six years and was President from 1988-90.

Shig Hirai (Nisei, born in Vancouver, BC, 1937) spent the war years in Lemon Creek, BC. In 1947 he was sent to Japan for schooling, and he returned to Canada in 1954. He has lived in Vancouver since 1957 and owns Fujiya, a Japanese food store, on Powell Street. A strong supporter of the Festival, he has operated a food booth since the first year.

Shinobu Homma (Ijusha, born in Niigata, Japan, 1952) immigrated to Canada in 1980. He was a member of Katari Taiko until he moved to Toronto in 1985. He performed at the Festival as well as volunteering during his years in Vancouver, and served as Site Coordinator in 1983. He is currently an architect in Toronto.

Toshimasa Ito (Ijusha, born in Shimabara, Nagasaki, Japan, 1947) came to Vancouver in 1972. His first involvement with the Festival was helping to construct the JCCA booth. Subsequently he became a regular volunteer, and acted as Site Coordinator for a number of years. He is a landscape architect and has a small firm in Richmond.

Diane Kadota (Sansei, born in Vancouver, BC, 1955) began her career as an agricultural journalist in Saskatoon. When she returned to Vancouver in 1986, she worked for the Asia Pacific Festival and Urbanarium. She coordinated the Powell Street Festival in 1988 and served as President of the Powell Street Festival Society from 1990 to 1991. At present she is involved in arts management and advocacy. Among the artists she represents are Uzume Taiko, Katari Taiko, Lola McLaughlin and Margo Kane.

Shirley Kakutani (Nisei/Sansei, born in Vancouver, BC, 1929) moved with her family to Notch Hill, BC, then to New Denver during the war years. She has been active in the Japanese Canadian community and served as Co-chair of the JCCA in 1977-78, when the Centennial celebrations were taking place. She has volunteered for many years at the Powell Street Festival.

Gordon Kayahara (Sansei, born in Toronto, Ontario, 1954) moved to British Columbia from Ontario in 1979 and has been a volunteer at the Festival since that time. He has been a member of the Powell Street Festival Society Board of Directors since his move to Vancouver in 1987, acting as President from 1987 to 1988. He was also a Director of the JCCA from 1987 to 1991. Gordon is a forest ecological consultant.

Roy Kiyooka (Nisei, born in Moose Jaw, Saskatchewan, 1926) is an artist, photographer, poet and musician. He has taught in art schools and universities in Calgary, Mexico, Edmonton, Regina, Montreal and, since 1970, in Vancouver. In 1975, wearing a green tuxedo, he received the Order of Canada in recognition of his contribution to the fine arts. He has performed at many Festivals as a poet and musician.

Lucy Komori (Sansei, born in Kamloops, BC, 1955) was a member of Katari Taiko from 1980 until her move to Toronto in 1985. She performed and volunteered at the Powell Street Festival and served as Coordinator in 1983. At present, Lucy is Marketing Manager at the University of Toronto School of Continuing Education.

Cathy Makihara (Sansei/Nisei, born in Vancouver, BC, 1963) was a field worker in the Japanese Canadian Redress Implementation Program sponsored by the National Association of Japanese Canadians as part of the Redress settlement. She coordinated the Powell Street Festival in 1989 and 1990 and serves on the Board of Directors. Cathy is currently the Administrator at Tonari Gumi.

Roy Miya (Nisei, born in Vancouver, BC, 1925) was interned in Kaslo, BC during World War Two. He is a sign painter and jazz pianist in Toronto and performed at the Festival in 1989. His album, *Saigon Dreaming*, came out in 1990.

Mami Miyata (Ijusha, born in Tokyo, Japan, 1951) came to Vancouver in 1975. She was Artistic Director of the Festival from 1979 to 1984 and was a member of its Board of Directors for six years. She is a freelance journalist and translator/interpreter.

Les Murata (Sansei, born in Winnipeg, Manitoba, 1948) moved to Nanaimo in 1980. Since settling in Vancouver in 1983, he has volunteered at the Powell Street Festival, acting as Site Coordinator for a number of years. He coordinated the Festival in 1986. Les is a carpenter.

Nobutsune David Murata (Ijusha, born in Japan, 1957) moved to Vancouver with his family in 1968. He coordinated the Festival in 1987. He is an ordained United Church minister and, at present, is community minister and Executive Director of the Jane Finch Ministry Outreach Program in Toronto.

Dick Nakamura (Nisei, born in Comox, BC, 1924) spent the war years in southern Alberta. During his career he served in three branches of the armed forces. When he retired, he was the Director of the Information Branch of the federal Department of Agriculture in Regina, Saskatchewan. He has been on the Board of Directors of the Inter-Cultural Association of Greater Victoria for the past twelve years. He organized the Vancouver Island Japanese Canadian Society to work for redress and is now a Director of the Japanese Canadian Redress Foundation.

Renee Rodin is a sometime writer/artist who owns and operates a bookstore, R2B2, which sponsors a continuing series of readings. She has attended the Powell Street Festival since 1977.

Michiko Sakata (Ijusha, born in Nagasaki, Japan, 1938) founded Language Aid, a social service agency that provided information, counselling, translation and interpretation services. This agency merged with another to become MOSAIC. Michiko also initiated the Japanese Canadian Centennial Project, *A Dream of Riches*, in 1976. She has been involved with Tonari Gumi since its inception as a volunteer and Director. Currently she owns a Japanese import and retail shop, Kaya Kaya.

Ken Shikaze (Sansei, born in Mission, BC, 1951) has been active in the Vancouver Japanese Canadian community since the Centennial year, working for the Powell Street Festival and Tonari Gumi. He was on the Festival's first Board of Directors and has served as the Volunteers' Coordinator. He also served as Executive Director for the National Nikkei Heritage Centre for two years.

Naomi Shikaze (Sansei, born in Lethbridge, Alberta, 1949) worked at Tonari Gumi when she returned to Vancouver in 1976 after two years in Japan. She was involved in the organization of the first Powell Street Festival. She coordinated the Festival in 1984 with Etsuko Yamanouchi, and, besides performing as a member of Katari Taiko, has served as Lottery Coordinator and Volunteers' Coordinator. At present, Naomi is the Volunteer Coordinator at Tonari Gumi.

Kyoshi Shimizu (Nisei, born in Kingcome Inlet, BC, 1920) spent the war years in Kaslo, Slocan, New Denver and Tashme. After the war she lived in Toronto and Ottawa. She was the first trained social worker in the Japanese Canadian community. When she retired in 1987, she moved to Vancouver and then to Victoria, where she is active in providing information on the development of small-group homes for the elderly.

Rick Shiomi (Sansei, born in Toronto, Ontario, 1947) coordinated the first Powell Street Festival in 1977, as well as those from 1979 to 1982. Subsequently, he moved to San Francisco, where his first play, *Yellow Fever*, was produced in 1983. *Yellow Fever* has since been presented in Los Angeles, New York and Toronto. He has written five plays and was a scriptwriter for the television series *ENG*. His most recent play, *Uncle Tadao*, opened in Los Angeles in January 1992.

Tom Shoyama (Nisei, born in Kamloops, BC, 1916) was interned in Kaslo during the war. He worked as a civil servant in Ottawa from 1964 to 1980, when he retired as Deputy Minister of Finance. He now lives in Victoria and is Visiting Professor to the School of Public Administration at the University of Victoria, Chairman of Atomic Energy of Canada and Constitutional Advisor to the Privy Council Office.

Mayu Takasaki (Sansei, born in Vancouver, BC, 1952) began working at Tonari Gumi on her return to Vancouver in 1977 after spending two and a half years in Kyoto. She has served on the JCCA and Tonari Gumi boards of directors. Mayu coordinated the 1978 Powell Street Festival and has provided administrative continuity for all the Festivals, as well as performing as a member of Katari Taiko. She is currently administrative assistant at Canaway Consultants and Kaya Kaya.

Bart Uchida (Sansei, born in Vancouver, BC, 1941) spent the war years in Taylor Lake, Christina Lake and Lone Butte, BC. After the war his family relocated to Hamilton, Ontario. A sculptor and performance artist, Bart moved to the United States in 1981. At present, as well as continuing his own work, he is an artist educator who works collaboratively with Boston inner-city school children. He performed at the Powell Street Festival in 1985 and 1988.

Terry Watada (Sansei, born in Toronto, Ontario, 1951) is a singer/songwriter with seven albums produced. He is a columnist for the *Nikkei Voice* and is writing a history of the Buddhist Church in Canada. His first play, *Dear Wes, Love Muriel*, was produced at the Earth Spirit Festival in 1991 at Harbourfront. He also teaches English at a college in Toronto. Terry has performed at all the Powell Street Festivals.

Les Yamada (Sansei, born in Montreal, Quebec, 1953) moved to Vancouver in 1980, first attended the Festival in 1982 and has gradually become more involved as a volunteer, helping to coordinate the food booths in 1991. He is a Client Supervisor working with the mentally handicapped.

Takeo Yamashiro (Ijusha, born in Hiroshima, Japan, 1943) immigrated to Vancouver in 1972. He founded Tonari Gumi with Jun Hamada in 1974 and has worked there since as the Director. Takeo first came up with the idea for the Powell Street Festival, and Tonari Gumi has been one of its strongest supporters. Takeo is a Master shakuhachi player and performed at the Festival for many years.

Ron Yamauchi (Sansei, born in Edmonton, Alberta, 1966) is a Human Rights Officer for the Canadian Human Rights Commission and also a freelance journalist, writing for such publications as the *Georgia Straight* and *Monday* magazine. He performed at the 1991 Powell Street Festival with his band.

ACKNOWLEDGEMENTS

It has taken the energy and creative talents of thousands of people to sustain fifteen years of the Powell Street Festival, and even though your images and thoughts may not appear on these pages, I am deeply indebted to all of you for making this book possible.

The original idea for the Festival came from the fertile imagination of Takeo Yamashiro. He and Tonari Gumi, the organization he heads, were also the first to make the commitment in 1977 to turn the idea into reality. At one point, the first Festival threatened to implode with the tensions between the young "radicals" and the traditional leadership, but Gordon Kadota, with his diplomatic skills and standing in the community, brought us together and saved the Festival. However, the real parents of the Festival are Rick Shiomi and Mayu Takasaki: they not only saw the Festival through its difficult birth but, more importantly, nursed it through the critical early years until its survival was assured. They have left a legacy of the Festival as an innovative and authentic expression of Nikkei culture.

In the years since those heady days of the 1977 Nikkei Centennial, people like Terry Watada, Pat Canning and especially Rick Shiomi have supported my work and insisted I bring this book to completion. Their encouragement finally resulted in the Sai Kai Project, whose objective was to produce a book and touring exhibit on the Festival. The directors of the Powell Street Festival Society voted to sponsor the project and since then they have not only been unstinting in their support, but also allowed us complete editorial and artistic freedom. The Sai Kai Project was launched successfully thanks to the administrative assistance of two exceptional people, Diane Kadota and Cathy Makihara. They have since gone on to fulfill other important roles in the rebuilding of our community and their duties have been placed in the capable hands of Patricia Canning.

Since the beginning, my partner and soul-mate in this project has been Linda Uyehara Hoffman. We first met back in 1976 when we worked together on *A Dream of Riches*, another book/exhibit that dealt with 100 years of Japanese Canadian history. Although Linda is a Sansei, she is the antithesis of the stereotypical shy, retiring Asian Canadian female. A photograph of Linda graces the cover of this book, and those who have watched her perform with Katari Taiko or heard her belt out the blues in a voice that ranges somewhere between Janis Joplin and Bessie Smith, have undoubtedly felt the force of this remarkable woman. That power, coupled with a keen intellect, enabled her to serve brilliantly as the oral histories editor for this book.

Linda not only conducted the lion's share of the interviews, she also edited all the final transcripts. Gathering the thoughts of nearly a hundred Festival participants was a prodigious task that took over a year, and Linda and I were most fortunate to have the able assistance of two people who have been mainstays of the Festival since day one. Terry Watada, teacher, writer and musician, interviewed a number of people in Toronto while Mami Miyata, one of the most insightful members of the new immigrant community, conducted interviews in Japanese. Two old friends, Maya Koizumi in Tokyo and Gordon Kadota, volunteered their professional skills to translate Mami's interviews.

The quality of a finished piece is dependent, first and foremost, on the quality of the original material, and I am most grateful to all of you who have taken the time to talk with Terry, Mami and Linda. Working with your thoughts, spoken with such eloquence, insight and refreshing honesty, has been both a privilege and a profound learning experience. My only regret is that only a small portion of this wealth of material could be included in this book.

I have also had the privilege and good fortune to work with an exceptional editorial team. Linda, of course, who fought stubbornly to preserve the integrity of the Festival vision and the authenticity of the voices she recorded. Paul Wong, whom we brought into the project later to act as curator for the exhibit and associate editor for this book. I have admired Paul for a long time, both as a creator and as an advocate for artists of colour. We wanted Paul to contextualize this work, to explore and place *Kikyō* within the crucial artistic, political and moral issues facing our society. In his essay, he has fulfilled this mandate with his usual brilliance. Mary Schendlinger, our editor at Harbour Publishing, demanded we give of ourselves and then, with consummate skill and sensitivity, helped to fine-tune our efforts into the best book that we were collectively capable of producing. When our work was completed, Roger Handling added the final grace note to *Kikyō* with his superb design.

My final thanks go to my wife, Mayu, who for the past six months has had to endure a totally preoccupied mate and a chaotic home flooded by hundreds of photos and reams of paper. I'm most grateful for her support and patience, which has allowed me to bring some semblance of order to this chaos.

Tamio Wakayama

歸鄉 歸鄉 歸鄉 歸鄉

歸鄉 歸鄉 歸鄉

歸鄉 歸鄉 歸鄉 歸鄉

歸鄉 歸鄉 歸鄉

歸鄉 歸鄉 歸鄉 歸鄉

歸鄉 歸鄉 歸鄉